The Blessing
of Taking
Communion

The Blessing of Taking Communion

Copyright © 2022 Breakfast for Seven

Produced and Distributed by Breakfast for Seven
2150 E. Continental Blvd., Southlake, TX 76092
breakfastforseven.com

Unless otherwise noted, all Scripture quotations are taken from the New King James Version®. Copyright © 1982 by Thomas Nelson. Used by permission. All rights reserved.

Scripture quotations marked TLB are taken from The Living Bible, copyright © 1971. Used by permission of Tyndale House Publishers, Inc., Carol Stream, Illinois 60188. All rights reserved.

Scripture quotations marked KJV are taken from the King James Version®. Public domain.

Scripture quotations marked TPT are taken from The Passion Translation®. Copyright © 2017, 2018, 2020 by Passion & Fire Ministries, Inc. Used by permission. All rights reserved. ThePassionTranslation.com.

Scripture quotations marked NLT are taken from the Holy Bible, New Living Translation, copyright © 1996, 2004, 2015 by Tyndale House Foundation. Used by permission of Tyndale House Publishers, Carol Stream, Illinois 60188. All rights reserved.

ISBN: 978-1-951701-30-7
ISBN: 978-1-951701-26-0 (eBook)

Printed in the United States of America.

The Blessing of Taking Communion

10 Guided Encounters At The Lord's Table

BREAKFAST
FOR **SEVEN**

TABLE OF CONTENTS

INTRODUCTION

Communion.

The way you approach this word probably depends on your upbringing and your church traditions.

Even the title of this sacrament varies from church to church, denomination to denomination, one stream of faith to another.

For some, it's the Eucharist. For others, it's the Holy Sacrament. And for many, it is simply the Lord's Supper.

The observance of it comes with variations as well.

You may have taken Communion weekly or only at Easter. It might have been the focal point of the service or perhaps only an afterthought.

Did you have grape juice or wine? Crackers, wafers, matzah, or bread? Did you stand in line and receive from the priest or, perhaps, serve one another as you passed the Communion tray?

Though our traditions are unique, there is one unfortunate common denominator among most who involve themselves in this historic component of the Christian faith . . . confusion.

Why exactly am I doing this? How often should I do this? Am I doing this right? Am I holy enough to do this? Am I old enough to do this? Am I in danger if I do this?

These are just a few of the questions, and if you've asked these or others, that's okay. You're not the only one who has wondered, questioned, been confused, or felt unworthy.

Most of us partake of Communion with an internal question mark rather than an exuberant exclamation point. It can feel ancient and mysterious. As though it has no real, modern-day value to us as believers.

We go along with the program simply because it's that time of the service or that day of the year. And most of us have never thought about taking Communion anywhere but church or in times of fellowship.

But what if we understood Communion on a deeper level? What if we were able to expose some of the misleadings, misunderstandings, and missed opportunities that await us by taking Communion? Would it change how we partake, or perhaps even how often we partake?

More importantly, how would it change our relationship with Jesus, the One who encouraged us to remember Him through Holy Communion?

The truth is that Communion is more than a break in the service; it is a balm for your soul, and it contains untapped blessing and power for your everyday life, your prayer life, and your intimacy with Jesus.

Communion was never meant to be a dutiful event, but rather a divine encounter . . . each time you partake of the bread and the wine.

Please let's not get caught up in wine or grape juice, wafers or crackers, leavened or unleavened bread. We are talking about the greatest exchange ever in the history of the world.

The great exchange is when Jesus gave His life, His body, and His blood and exchanged them so that you might enjoy life, health, and forgiveness in Him.

In the pages of this book, you'll discover a greater understanding of what those encounters mean and how they can impact every aspect of your life and the lives of those around you.

As you read these words — as you begin this book — know this . . .

God's gifts are waiting for you. Grace is being poured out on you. Mercy is chasing you down. You're already forgiven. You can never become more righteous than you are today. Your body can be made whole. Your mind can be renewed. Your behavior has not disqualified you. Jesus' sacrifice has qualified you forever. You are now loved forever by your heavenly Father.

And it's all because of the finished work of God's Son.

Communion reminds, reinforces, and puts in motion the promises of His sacrifice. It's so much more than a ceremony, it's a celebration — more than a tradition, it's a transformation.

Let's discover how together.

The Blessing
of Taking
Communion

Let us therefore come boldly to the throne of grace, that we may obtain mercy and find grace to help in time of need.

HEBREWS 4:16

CHAPTER ONE

Mercy, Grace, and Righteousness Encounter

Fiorello La Guardia famously served as the mayor of New York City from 1934 to 1945. A story is told of him showing up at night court one brutally cold January night, dismissing the sitting judge, and presiding over the criminal cases himself.

A case number was rattled off, and a woman who was accused of stealing bread from a local grocery store was brought before the court.

When given a chance to state her defense, the haggard mother pled guilty, explaining why she had committed the crime — her husband had deserted her, her daughter was sick, and her grandchildren were hungry.

The owner of the grocery store was in attendance that night to press charges. "It's a bad neighborhood, your Honor," the owner said. "She has to be punished to teach other people around here a lesson."

La Guardia thought a minute before rendering his sentence. Justice was required and there was no doubt the woman was guilty of the crime.

"I have to punish you," the mayor, turned judge, proclaimed. "The law makes no exceptions. Ten dollars or ten days in jail."

But even as La Guardia declared his sentence, the courtroom fell to a hush as he reached into his own pocket and extracted a ten-dollar bill. "Here is the ten-dollar fine which I now remit."[i]

The application here is easy: We are the woman who has committed a crime. We've messed up in our lives. We're guilty. Justice demands a verdict.

The difference is that we don't even need an accuser present to point out our indiscretions, we know them full well. We remind ourselves daily of what we've done, how we've failed, when we've let others down, and why we're deserving of punishment and not forgiveness.

But the beauty of the gospel is that rather than demand we pay for our sins, Jesus paid for them Himself. On the cross of Calvary, God's mercy provided what His own justice demanded.

Isaiah, under the inspiration of the Holy Spirit, prophesied about Christ's substitutionary atonement some 700 years before Jesus' day of sacrifice. He wrote of Jesus:

> But He was wounded for our transgressions, He was bruised for our iniquities; the chastisement for our peace was upon Him, and by His stripes we are healed . . . and the LORD has laid on Him the iniquity of us all. (Isaiah 53:5–6)

And when Jesus instituted Communion, or what is referred to as the Lord's Supper, the Bible says:

> Then He took the cup, and gave thanks, and gave it to them, saying, "Drink from it, all of you. For this is My blood of the new covenant, which is shed for many for the remission of sins." (Matthew 26:27–28)

Remittance is payment. When Jesus shed His blood, when He gave His life, He made full and final payment for the forgiveness of the sins of the whole world.

You're not stained; you're not guilty. Isaiah 1:18 says:

> "Come now, and let us reason together," says the Lord, "though your sins are like scarlet, they shall be as white as snow; though they are red like crimson, they shall be as wool."

When we partake of the cup in Holy Communion, we're reminded of God's mercy — that we did not have to pay the penalty we deserved.

When God looks at you, He doesn't see your faults and flaws, He sees the righteousness of His Son Jesus.

We're reminded of His grace — that which He has given that we don't deserve.

Favor, peace, joy, abundance, blessings, healing, unconditional love. In and of ourselves, we didn't deserve any of these things, but God's grace lavishes them upon us freely. They were His. He gave them up at the cross, so that we, as believers, can enjoy them now and in the life to come.

Grace and mercy would be enough. In fact, it would be more than enough. But the finished work of Jesus on the cross provided something else . . . righteousness. 2 Corinthians 5:21 says:

> For He made Him who knew no sin to be sin for us, that we might become the righteousness of God in Him.

You are more than a forgiven sinner — this verse tells you that you are the very righteousness of God because you are in Christ Jesus.

When God looks at you, He doesn't see your faults and flaws, He sees the righteousness of

His Son Jesus. Isaiah 61:10 says that you are clothed in the robe of righteousness.

The Communion encounter declares to you who you really are. In Christ Jesus, you are forgiven, loved, redeemed, restored, and righteous. When you embrace that encounter, it changes the way you approach your heavenly Father.

You're not unworthy, begging for crumbs. No, you are righteous in His sight. You can come to Him anytime, anywhere, for whatever you need — because He delights in you. Hebrews 4:16 says:

> Let us therefore come boldly to the throne of grace, that we may obtain mercy and find grace to help in time of need.

What do you need from your heavenly Father today? Do you need wisdom for an important decision? Are you longing for peace? Is there a dream in your heart that you have given up on? Does your body need healing? Does your soul need rest?

Whatever you need, the work of Jesus has provided. Ask daily. Pray fearlessly. Come boldly and take Communion as an expression of receiving these precious gifts that have been given to you.

 **Prayer**

Father, I thank You for the sacrifice of Your Son Jesus on the cross. When accusations come from without or within, help me to remember what Jesus provided for me on the cross. Because of Your mercy, my debt has been paid, and I am forgiven of my sins. Your grace provides every spiritual blessing. Because You love me, there is no good thing You will withhold from me.

Declaration

I come to this table expectant. I take this bread, thankful that Your body, Jesus, took my punishment because of Your love and mercy for me. I drink this cup, remembering that the shedding of Your blood has made me righteous and allows me to boldly enter the throne room of grace.

My heavenly Father has taken away my garments of sin and shame and dressed me in the robe of righteousness that Jesus provided through His perfect, finished work. I receive the promises in God's Word, and I choose to see myself the way He sees me — forgiven, redeemed, restored, highly favored, loved unconditionally, and in unbroken and eternal fellowship with Him.

Who Himself bore our sins in His own body on the tree, that we, having died to sins, might live for righteousness — by whose stripes you were healed.

1 PETER 2:24

CHAPTER TWO

The Passover Healing Encounter

Are you dealing with a sickness or an illness? Is your body weary or your mind unsettled? If so, there is a healing encounter for you when you receive Communion. It was foreshadowed in the Old Testament and fulfilled in the sacrifice of Jesus.

Luke 22 and Matthew 26 give us accounts of the Lord's Supper. It's important to understand that when Jesus broke the bread and poured the wine in the upper room that night, it was not an ordinary dinner.

It was the Passover celebration. Instituted in Exodus 12, Passover is the annual Jewish feast to commemorate the deliverance of the Jewish people from bondage.

The disciples surely understood the significance of this meal, as all Jewish people did. But what they didn't yet understand was the parallel of Jesus' work on the cross and God's deliverance of His people from Egypt.

The Old Testament tells us that the Israelites had been slaves in Egypt for 430 years. For generations, oppression was all they knew. But in Exodus 3, God raised up a leader, Moses, to lead them out of Egypt and into the Promised Land of Israel.

God told Moses, "I have surely seen the oppression of My people" (v. 7), and "I have come down to deliver them out of the hand of the Egyptians" (v. 8).

When Moses confronted Pharaoh, demanding "Let My people go," it was met with opposition. (Deliverance always is.) Pharaoh refused to release his hold on God's people.

In Exodus 7–10, we read of nine plagues that came upon the Egyptians and their gods due to their disobedience to God's command, and in chapter 12, the final plague — the death of the firstborn in every household — was unleashed.

To protect the Israelites, God instructed Moses to have His people put the blood of a spotless lamb on the doors of their dwellings. When the angel of death saw the blood of the lamb, he would "pass over" that home. Exodus 12:13 says:

> "Now the blood shall be a sign for you on the houses where you are. And when I see the blood, I will pass over you; and the plague shall not be on you to destroy you when I strike the land of Egypt."

God also told Moses to have the people pack unleavened bread for the journey out of Egypt. Verse 11 says:

> "And thus you shall eat it: with a belt on your waist, your sandals on your feet, and

your staff in your hand. So you shall eat it in haste. It is the LORD's Passover."

The sacrifice of a lamb. Protection under the blood. Provision for the journey. This was a fore-shadow of the new covenant in Jesus.

In Matthew 26, Jesus, the Bread of Life, broke the bread and told His disciples, *"Take, eat; this is My body."* In the next moment, Jesus, the Lamb of God, poured the wine and said,

> "Drink from it, all of you. For this is My blood of the new covenant, which is shed for many for the remission of sins." (vv. 26–28)

What was foreshadowed had now been fulfilled. His body broken. His blood shed. And now we can freely access His provision and protection.

We are able to walk whole and healed by the stripes of our Savior. His sacrifice provided for your mental, emotional, and physical health.

There is a grace note in Scripture about the Passover that any who are sick, tired, oppressed, or infirmed can cling to. Psalm 105:37 (TLB) says:

. . . and brought his people safely out from Egypt, loaded with silver and gold; there were no sick and feeble folk among them.

Scholars estimate that between two and three million Israelites left Egypt. And despite years of servitude and oppression, Scripture tells us that "there were no sick and feeble" that night.

They walked out of bondage strong, safe, supplied, healthy, and whole. No lack, no sickness, no attack.

These are the promises God has for you. And Communion is an act of worship and receiving that reminds us of these promises and often sets our faith in motion.

To take the Lord's Supper is not only to receive God's forgiveness but to receive the life He promised, the healing He promised, the fresh start

He offered the Israelites then and the one He offers you today — spirit, soul, and body. Isaiah 53:5 says:

> But He was wounded for (your) transgressions, He was bruised for (your) iniquities; the chastisement for (your) peace was upon Him, and by His stripes (you) are healed.

It's not a wishful thought or a spiritual platitude. We are able to walk whole and healed by the stripes of our Savior. His sacrifice provided for your mental, emotional, and physical health.

And let's be clear here, this is not saying you will never have a headache or a fever. Psalm 34:19 tells us,

> Many are the afflictions of the righteous, but the LORD delivers him out of them all.

Jesus would not have provided for healing in the new covenant if healing was never going to be needed.

So, let me ask you again: *Are you experiencing a sickness or an illness? Is your body weary or your mind unsettled and even depressed?*

If so, be reminded of Christ's healing work on the cross when you receive Communion. Let that flood your heart with hope and, with great faith, receive from your heavenly Father complete health and wholeness.

In the same way God saw the oppression of His people in Egypt, He has surely seen the burden and oppression of your illness. And He has come down to deliver you. There is a healing encounter for you at the Communion table. When you partake of the bread, representing His body that was broken for you, you are partaking of His health, His life, His gift of healing. You cannot do anything to deserve it, His broken body was His gift to you for your healing and wholeness.

Prayer

Father, thank You that Your Son, Jesus, bore my sin and my sickness on the cross. His body was broken for me and His blood was shed for me that I may live a healthier life on the Earth and eternally with You in Heaven. I do not have to live with the same sicknesses and diseases of the world because the blood of Jesus, the Lamb of God, covers and protects me. I thank You for new strength, increased energy, a clear mind, and a restored body. Today, I receive Your healing work in every area of my life.

Declaration

I take this bread and receive my healing. Because of Jesus' broken body, I can be healthy and whole. Just as the unleavened bread of the first Passover was broken, and afterward, the vast Israelite nation left Egypt with none sick or feeble, so this bread reminds me that supernatural wholeness is mine through Jesus' sacrifice.

I drink this cup and choose to be at peace. The blood of Jesus is my covering and my protection. It reminds me of the blood of the Passover lamb painted on the Israelite doorposts that provided complete protection from harm. Jesus' shed blood is painted on the doorposts of my life, my mind, my soul, and my body.

For when we were still without strength, in due time Christ died for the ungodly. For scarcely for a righteous man will one die; yet perhaps for a good man someone would even dare to die. But God demonstrates His own love toward us, in that while we were still sinners, Christ died for us. Much more then, having now been justified by His blood, we shall be saved from wrath through Him.

For if when we were enemies we were reconciled to God through the death of His Son, much more, having been reconciled, we shall be saved by His life. And not only that, but we also rejoice in God through our Lord Jesus Christ, through whom we have now received the reconciliation.

ROMANS 5:6–11

CHAPTER THREE

Torn Veil Encounter

The creation story started so beautifully. When we read it now, it's almost too perfect to comprehend. Adam and Eve were in daily, unbroken fellowship with the very God who breathed His life into them.

A garden with limitless provision and unspeakable beauty. A paradise designed by the Creator and shared with His creation. Adam and Eve walked daily in the cool of the garden with God Himself. No sadness. No war. No disease. No shame. No fear.

When sin entered the story, it stained and changed all of that. The moment man chose temptation over trust, the story was tragically altered. Fallen humanity could no longer have perfect fellowship with a holy God. Shame, fear, anxiety, sadness, and so much more were felt for the first time.

There are many consequences of sin, but the one that made the earth groan and humanity ache was separation from God.

The Old Testament is an account of that groan and that ache. Fallen man striving to reach a holy God through a prescribed means — rituals, animal sacrifices, good works, prophets, and priests.

It is perhaps best seen by the veil in the temple that separated the people from the holy of holies. Only the High Priest, on the Day of Atonement, and only with a blood sacrifice, could access the presence of God.

But because of His relentless love, God sent His Son to bridge the chasm of sin that separated us from Him. **Jesus lived a sinless life in order to be a perfect sacrifice.** His death atoned for our sins and erased our shame.

Mark 15:37–38 tells us what happened in the temple when Jesus finished His work on the cross . . .

> And Jesus cried out with a loud voice, and breathed His last. Then the veil of the temple was torn in two from top to bottom.

The veil — the very thing that limited access to God — was torn from top to bottom. Jesus, our perfect High Priest, made the ultimate sacrifice so that we could once again be in daily, unbroken relationship with our heavenly Father. There was now no more separation between God and man, ever.

"Let us draw near." Because of Jesus, we can once again say those words. We don't have to be good enough, we don't have to offer a sacrifice, we don't have to rely on a priest . . . we can simply draw near to our Father "by a new and living way which He consecrated for us."

Something powerful happens when we take Communion with a focus on Jesus rather than a focus on ourselves. It's a "torn veil" encounter where we remember that we are no longer separated from God. The body and blood of Jesus, which He willingly sacrificed, restored the closeness that sin stole so long ago. Now, we can once again walk in daily fellowship with our Creator.

Even the way we take Communion reminds us that we are no longer separated from God. You don't have to be in an ornate sanctuary to take Communion. You don't have to wait for a pastor or priest to take Communion. You don't even have to have juice and crackers, or wine and bread, to take Communion.

Rituals do not create relationship. Jesus has become our High Priest. We can come boldly before the throne of grace.

That means you can take Communion in your church on a Sunday morning and in your living room on a Monday afternoon. You can take Communion to receive healing on your way to a doctor's appointment. You can gather your family around the dining room table and take Communion together. You can ask co-laborers at

Rituals do not create relationship. Jesus has become our High Priest. We can come boldly before the throne of grace.

the office to gather with you and believe God for breakthroughs, healings, and answered prayers as you remember the sacrifice and the great exchange that Jesus offers us at the Lord's Table.

The veil is torn. The story is beautiful again. Let us draw near.

 **Prayer**

Father, because of Jesus' perfect redemptive work through His death and resurrection, I thank You that I am never separated from You. Your unconditional love pursues me and tells me that I am Yours. When I feel distant or alone, I pray that You will remind me that I can always draw near to You — that there is no power or principality that can keep me from You. Help me to quit disqualifying myself from Your goodness and grace. The veil has been torn and I know that I can have eternal, unbroken relationship with You.

Declaration

I take this bread, communing with my heavenly Father in a new and living way which He consecrated for me, through the veil, that is, His flesh. His broken body is my "way" back. Back to the Garden of Eden. Back to the Tree of Life. Back to . . . You.

I drink this cup, thankful that Jesus is my High Priest, and I can come before the Father anytime, fully qualified, because of the blood Jesus shed for the remission of my sins.

That blood has cleansed me of all guilt, all shame, all condemnation, and all that stood between me and Him. I come now and forever with confidence. I come boldly to the throne of grace and receive supernatural help for every need.

Therefore, brethren, having boldness to enter the Holiest by the blood of Jesus, by a new and living way which He consecrated for us, through the veil, that is, His flesh, and having a High Priest over the house of God, let us draw near with a true heart in full assurance of faith, having our hearts sprinkled from an evil conscience and our bodies washed with pure water.

HEBREWS 10:19–22

CHAPTER FOUR

The New Covenant in His Blood Encounter

Anytime you book a flight, rent a car, stay in a hotel, or make a purchase, there are two words that are hard to resist: *free upgrade.*

• Ma'am, economy class is full, but don't worry, we're giving you a free upgrade to first class. *Is that okay?*

• Sir, we're running a promotion and offering you a larger room at no cost. *Do you mind?*

• Ma'am, we're out of compact cars. So, we're upgrading you to a luxury vehicle. *Will that be satisfactory?*

• Sir, we're actually offering a two-for-one sale today. *Would you like to pick out another for free?*

Maybe after some initial skepticism, our answers are easy: Yes. Yes. Yes. Yes. **Why settle for less when something new and better has been offered?**

I bring it up because "new" and "better" are words of promise that Scripture uses when talking about the new covenant Jesus established.

When Jesus served Communion at the Lord's Supper, he said: *"This is My blood of the new covenant, which is shed for many"* (Mark 14:24). And Hebrews tells us that this "new covenant" is a better covenant:

> But now He has obtained a more excellent ministry, inasmuch as He is also Mediator of a better covenant, which was established on better promises. Hebrews 8:6

If Jesus came to establish a new and better covenant, why would we live in anything less? Why would we continue to go back to the old as if it was the new?

The old covenant was a law-based covenant that God established with the Israelites on Mount Sinai after leading them out of Egypt.

This covenant came with conditions — blessings or curses that were the results of obedience or disobedience. Laws were given to reveal to us our sin and make us more aware of our need for God.

In the old covenant, it was *man's* good deeds, *man's* sacrifices, and *man's* adherence to the law that kept judgment away. It was a covenant built on struggle, merit, law, and the sacrifice of animals.

And under the old covenant, there was a constant striving to be good enough in order to achieve right standing before God.

The old covenant may have been established thousands of years ago on Mount Sinai, but many in the church are still trying (and failing) to live under its demands.

God did not send His son to restore us to good behavior. He sent Jesus to restore us to Himself! Yet, too often, we try to earn God's approval by the things we do or avoid doing. We struggle to be good enough. And we're frustrated and ashamed when we're not.

We count our sins and assume God is disappointed, angry, and has definitely disqualified us from receiving anything good. *Surely, God can't be pleased with me, we think. I'm not even pleased with myself. How could God hear my prayer? Why would God bless my life?*

But John 1:17 tells us that Jesus ushered in a new covenant. A covenant not based in law but built on grace. John tells us:

> For the law was given through Moses, but grace and truth came through Jesus Christ.

God did not send His son to restore us to good behavior. He sent Jesus to restore us to Himself!

Under the new covenant — a new and better covenant — the blood of Jesus met every demand of the law. He met every condition and requirement for blessing from God.

We no longer have to strive for perfection because Jesus was perfect in our place. We're not righteous or unrighteous based on our good works; we're forever in right standing before God because of Jesus' finished work.

Hebrews 8:13 says that when Jesus established the new covenant, He rendered the old covenant "obsolete." And in the very next chapter, it says that *"Christ came as High Priest of the good things to come, with the greater and more perfect tabernacle not made with hands, that is, not of this creation"* (Hebrews 9:11).

You don't have to expect lack, rejection, defeat, or failure. As a new covenant believer, you can have a joyful expectation of *"the good things to come."*

The sacrifice of Jesus that we remember each time we take Communion has not only provided for our eternity in Heaven, it has opened the door for us to partake of God's goodness here on Earth.

God's favor, provision, healing, wisdom, peace, joy, strength — all this (and so much more) is yours under the "better" new covenant in Jesus Christ.

And do you know what it costs you? Nothing. It's free. It was all bought and paid for by the blood of Jesus.

Your life hasn't just been upgraded — it's been uplifted. Your back is no longer bent by the heaviness of the law. The blood of our Savior has freed you from shame's burden and elevated you to the very righteousness of God in Christ Jesus.

Are you ready to walk in this new and better covenant? It's already been paid for. Imagine Jesus going through what He did, knowing the price he was paying for our future, our new life, and us refusing to receive it. May it never be.

 **Prayer**

Father, thank You for the new covenant relationship I can have with You in Christ Jesus. You've lifted the weight of guilt and shame from my life. I no longer have to live under the old covenant of law. Because of the blood Jesus shed for me, I can now live in the new covenant of grace. When I try to earn Your approval by my own good works, help me to remember that the finished work of Jesus is all I need. Help me receive Your new and better covenant and live in the beauty of your promises today and every day from this point forward.

Declaration

I take this bread in grateful, joyful recognition that Jesus, the Bread of Life, came to completely satisfy every requirement of the law on my behalf; and therefore, I qualify for every promise in God's Word. I stand in Jesus' qualification for material and spiritual blessing. In eating, I recognize that I am in Him and He is in me.

I drink this cup in grateful and joyful recognition that Jesus' blood inaugurated and sealed a new covenant connecting me to the Father. It is a better covenant, established on better promises. The old covenant is obsolete and has passed away. In the new one, I'm fully righteous and completely restored. Through the blood of this new covenant, provision, healing, wisdom, peace, joy, strength, and much more are mine.

Behold, how good and how pleasant it is for brethren to dwell together in unity!

PSALM 133:1

CHAPTER FIVE

The Body of Christ
Unity Encounter

There are many differences in the body of Christ. All you have to do is visit the local churches in your community to see that.

Some churches like the lights low and the contemporary music loud. Others prefer the sun to stream in through stained glass windows and the sound of treasured hymns.

Some pastors thunder passionately, inspiring and emboldening us. Others preach in a conversational tone, causing us to ponder and reflect.

Topical. Expository. Liturgical. Contemporary. Long services. Short services. Loud music. Soft music. Exuberance. Reflection. Instruments. A cappella.

Our denominations are varied. Our traditions are unique. Our viewpoints are unalike. At our best, we are beautifully diverse. At our worst, we are bitterly divided.

The apostle Paul worried about this division. He wrote in his first letter to the Corinthians:

> Now I plead with you, brethren, by the name of our LORD Jesus Christ, that you all speak the same thing, and that there be no divisions among you, but that you be perfectly joined together in the same mind and in the same judgment. 1 Corinthians 1:10

And it is in Communion that the apostle's pleading and the Scriptures' command for unity are heard, observed, and obeyed.

Because at the Lord's Table, our differences are forgotten and our divisions are healed. When we take Communion, however we take it, we are all remembering the body of Christ broken for us and His blood shed for the forgiveness of our sins.

We may disagree on eschatology, worship styles, or preferred Bible translations, but all of us who call Jesus our Savior celebrate His sacrifice that delivered us from our sins and gave us new life in Him.

And Holy Communion doesn't just unite us with other believers; it connects us with past generations of believers — the saints of old and the great cloud of witnesses who went before us in faith.

At the Table of the Lord, we participate in the same sacred moment in which every other generation of Jesus followers throughout history has engaged.

The bread and the cup unite us with those first Jesus followers, telling His story from eyewitness accounts. It unites us with the earliest martyrs and persecuted saints, singing hymns and breaking bread in catacombs and caves. It connects us to history's missionaries who left the comforts of home and family to take the gospel to unreached people groups in faraway places.

The table connects us to families huddled in bunkers during world wars; men and women sailing to new lands in search of religious freedom; packed crowds under revival tents — they've all taken the same elements that we do today to remember the miraculous and compassionate acts of Jesus.

And it unites us with the persecuted believers of our time, who risk all to call upon the name of Jesus. Oh, what a holy and powerful moment this truly is!

If you think about it, we're not as different or divided as some would accuse. We're all saved by faith, not by works. We were all far from God but brought near through the perfect sacrifice of Jesus. We can all now come boldly to Him before His throne of grace.

We are all welcome
at the Lord's Table,
and we are all unified
when we take the
bread and drink
from the cup.

John 3:16 (KJV) is perhaps the most quoted verse in all the Bible. It tells us:

> For God so loved the world, that He gave His only begotten Son, that whosoever believeth in Him should not perish, but have everlasting life.

Whosoever. What a beautiful, unifying word.

The believer who has been saved for decades is a "whosoever." The sinner kneeling at the altar is a "whosoever." The person who votes for a party other than yours is a "whosoever." The church that worships differently is full of "whosoevers."

We are all welcome at the Lord's Table, and we are all unified when we take the bread and drink from the cup. His body, the bread, His blood, the wine, are elements of the Christian faith that we cherish and can experience unity through.

The next time you take Communion — whether it's in your kitchen, in a hospital room, in a church service, or in your car on the way to work — remember that you are part of the body of Christ.

In Christ, we are unified. Not because of anything we have done. But because of what He has done. Each of us has been forgiven freely and loved unconditionally.

And this divine love that we all receive, or in the words of the apostle Paul, the love with which we are all "clothed," does something beautiful:

Above all, clothe yourselves with love, which binds us all together in perfect harmony. And let the peace that comes from Christ rule in your hearts. For as members of one body you are called to live in peace. And always be thankful. Colossians 3:14–15, NLT

Prayer

Father, what a joy it is to know that I'm not alone. Not only are You always with me, but I am unified with my brothers and sisters in Christ every time I partake of Communion. Thank You that I am part of Your body that is made up of many parts. Help me to look past differences in traditions or opinions and see others with love, the same way You see them and the way that You see me.

Declaration

I take this bread, representing Christ's broken body, with a deep sense of awareness that my connection to Him connects me to a vast "body" of believers . . . past, present, and future. I recognize that Jesus prayed that we would be "one" in the same way He and His Father were and are "one." I recognize that we are responsible for one another in love. I am a part of something far, far bigger than myself.

I take this cup, symbolizing the sinless blood of Jesus, shed not only for me but for all who have said "yes" to God's gracious offer of forgiveness, mercy, and restoration in Him.

I recognize that this blood not only clothes us in Jesus' own righteousness but also clothes us in divine, supernatural love for one another. And that Jesus said that this love for one another would be the signature mark of His followers.

And He took bread, gave thanks and broke it, and gave it to them, saying, "This is My body which is given for you; do this in remembrance of Me."

LUKE 22:19

CHAPTER SIX

Remembrance of Jesus Encounter

What a scene it must have been. Jesus — the healer, teacher, rabbi, Messiah — serving wine and bread to His disciples mere hours before He would be arrested, falsely tried, and crucified.

It was the Last Supper, but the only One who knew it was the Last Supper was Jesus.

The disciples couldn't fathom what was about to happen. The crowds in Jerusalem had no idea what would transpire. Mary didn't know her son was about to be poured out as a drink offering.

But Jesus knew. And with the weight of a sinful world beginning to bear down on Him, He made a simple, heartfelt request to His disciples: *Don't forget me.*

> "This is My body which is given for you; do this in remembrance of Me." Luke 22:19

In the moment, it must have seemed like a strange request. *Why is Jesus telling us to remember Him? How could we forget Him? What does remembering Jesus have to do with this Passover meal?*

Two millennia later, it might still seem like a strange request. Obviously, we haven't forgotten all that Jesus did. We know the stories, we read about the miracles, we recite the sermons.

But when Jesus uttered those words, He wasn't instructing His followers to remember who He was or what He did. He was telling us all to remember who He is and what He does.

Jesus and His finished work aren't constrained to the past. He is the great I Am. He told us Himself in John 14:6:

"I am the way, the truth, and the life. No one comes to the Father except through Me."

He told us to remember who He is and what He does, because we forget so easily, don't we? Yes we do, and Communion is an act of worship that brings us back to center, resetting our day and our beliefs to be in line with His promises, and His new covenant, His better covenant.

It's easy to get so caught up in the stress, worry, and busyness of daily life that we take our eyes off Jesus and think we're left to fend for ourselves.

Even the most fervent Christian can fall into the trap of trying to fix our own problems, prove our goodness to God, hide our pain, and spend sleepless nights worrying about an outcome.

But at the Lord's Table, when we partake of Communion, it's a holy moment where we can turn our attention, our real selves, back to Jesus and remember who He is and what He does.

The work of Jesus on the cross of Calvary provided everything we need. It's not something we have to do on our own; it's something we *receive* from Him.

Jesus is your peace. He is your joy. He is your provision. He is your righteousness. He is your healing. He is your favor. He is your waymaker. He is your advocate. He is your EVERYTHING. And when you partake of Communion, you are saying, "I want it all, Jesus. All of You and all that You purchased for me."

It's interesting that this isn't the only time the Bible implores us to remember all that God has provided. Psalm 103:2–5 says:

Bless the LORD, O my soul, and forget not all His benefits: who forgives all your iniquities, who heals all your diseases, who redeems your life from destruction, who crowns you with lovingkindness and tender mercies, who satisfies your mouth with good things, so that your youth is renewed like the eagle's.

The work of Jesus on the cross of Calvary provided everything we need. It's not something we have to do on our own; it's something we *receive* from Him.

Think about the blessing and power of those words — those promises. Forgiveness, healing, redemption, love, kindness, mercy, good things, renewed youth.

These are benefits too good to forget.

- When you find yourself in a predicament and it seems like there is no way out, remember that He has made a way where there seems to be no way.

- If you get a diagnosis that has you feeling worried or afraid, remember that by His stripes you are healed.

- On a day when your mind is filled with anxious thoughts and you feel a sense of dread, remember that He offers a peace and a hope that surpasses all understanding.

- When the bills are piling up, prices are rising, and your income doesn't look like enough, remember that He supplies all of your needs according to His riches in glory.

- In the moment you disappoint yourself and feel like you've let God down, remember that your righteousness is not through your own good works, but through His perfect work.

Communion is an encounter where you can look to Jesus and remember all of the gifts, promises, and benefits He has freely made available to you.

Mark 16:19 tells us when Jesus ascended into Heaven after His resurrection, that He *"sat down at the right hand of God."*

Sitting is a position of rest. He rests at the right hand of the Father because the work is finished. Everything you'll ever need has been provided for you. All that is left now for you to do is believe (John 6:29).

Prayer

Father, when life is overwhelming and when I'm easily distracted by busyness, help me remember all that Jesus did for me through His death and resurrection. I want to take my focus off of myself and my abilities. I want to fix my eyes on Jesus and His perfect, abundant, complete, and finished work on the cross. Let me never forget You will make a way, let me never forget I am healed, and let me never forget that You supply all my needs. For Your love, Your grace, and Your perfect supply are everything I need. Jesus, You are my everything.

Declaration

Jesus, as I take this bread, I remember ... YOU. I remember the kindness, gentleness, compassion, and healing power You displayed every day of Your earthly ministry. I remember how You called me ... by name ... and saved me and made me new. I remember how lost and hopeless I was before I surrendered my life to You. So I take this bread, which represents Your body, broken for me, with overflowing gratitude.

I drink this cup with my eyes fixed on Jesus, the One who began my journey of faith and the One who is committed to seeing it through ... to bring me victorious and whole into the presence of the Father. I remember His shed blood purchased me. I remember that it cleansed me for all time, making me pure and holy and blameless before my heavenly Father. I will not focus on my own flaws and weaknesses. My eyes are on Him and on His finished work on my behalf.

And as they were eating, Jesus took bread, blessed and broke it, and gave it to the disciples and said, "Take, eat; this is My body."

MATTHEW 26:26

CHAPTER SEVEN

Communing with Jesus Encounter

Have you ever looked forward to seeing someone or spending time with them? I mean, *really* looked forward to it?

Maybe it was a long-awaited family reunion, and you were going to see family members you hadn't seen in years. Or perhaps a lifelong friend was visiting from out of town, and you couldn't wait to catch up.

For those anticipated moments of fellowship, time seems to drag. Minutes feel like hours, and days feel like years. We're just so excited to spend time with the ones we love.

Jesus knows how that feels too.

Luke 22:14–15 gives us the picture of a Savior who couldn't wait to spend time with His disciples. It says:

> When the hour had come, He sat down, and the twelve apostles with Him. Then He said to them, "With fervent desire I have desired to eat this Passover with you before I suffer."

The Passion Translation says it this way . . .

> When Jesus arrived at the upper room, he took his place at the table along with all the apostles. Then he told them, "I have longed with passion and desire to eat this Passover lamb with you before I endure my sufferings."

Even with His crucifixion drawing near, Jesus' thoughts were on fellowship. He had a fervent desire — a passion — to spend time with His disciples in Communion.

Jesus had eaten many meals with these men over the previous three years, but He looked forward to this one with anticipation. That tells us something about taking Communion.

When you come to the Lord's Table, it is a special time to meet with Jesus. A time He is passionate about because He is passionate about His people. And He is passionate about you. It is a time of great expectation.

As a Christian, it is easy to fall into the mindset that says, *I need to love God more. I've got to spend more time reading the Bible; I've got to pray longer; I've got to serve more. That's how I'll show the Lord how much I love Him.*

Reading the Bible, spending time in prayer, serving others — these are wonderful things. But they aren't meant to be dutiful works we do in order to "love God enough."

The beautiful truth is that our relationship with God is not based on our love for Him. It never has been. Our relationship with God

is based on His love for us. We see this demonstrated all throughout Scripture.

God loved the Israelites, though they were doubting, grumbling, and complaining right after He delivered them from bondage in Egypt. Jesus talked of the Father who ran to welcome the Prodigal Son who had walked away. Paul was attacking and imprisoning Christians when Jesus met him on the Damascus Road and offered salvation.

In these examples, and so many more, God's love is pursuing people — relentless and unconditional. First John 4:10 says it this way:

> In this is love, not that we loved God, but that He loved us and sent His Son to be the propitiation for our sins.

When Jesus broke the bread and poured the wine at the Lord's Supper, He had fervently longed for that time of communion with His disciples.

He still fervently longs for times of communion with you.

The beautiful truth is
that our relationship
with God is not based
on our love for Him!
It never has been!
Our relationship with
God is based on
His love for us!

To take the bread and drink the cup is to have an encounter simply communing with Jesus. To know that you don't have to be good enough or love well enough. And the reason is profound: Jesus was good enough and loved well enough for you.

Every interaction and moment of relationship we have with Him is based on His love, not ours. He is looking forward to meeting you in Communion. Beloved one, He can't wait to see you there.

 **Prayer**

Father, thank You that You love me perfectly and unconditionally. The fact that You want to spend time with me is a beautiful display of Your goodness and Your kindness. Help me to set aside my agenda or any thoughts that I have to be good enough to receive Your love. I want to meet with You and share my questions, my fears, and my insecurities because I know You can calm them all. Your love is constantly pursuing me. So Jesus, let me get caught. Let me not run from your love but turn, face it, and receive it in abundance. Thank You. My relationship with You is built on Your love, Your sacrifice, and Your pursuit of me.

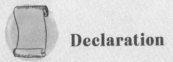

Declaration

Jesus, as I take this bread, representing Your broken body, I stand in awe of the privilege of knowing You. I marvel at the truth that You are more than my Savior-Redeemer... You are more than my Mighty King. You are my elder brother. You are my friend. In this holy moment, we are together. In this sacred space, I come to know You better.

Jesus, as I drink this cup that represents Your precious blood, I'm mindful that it has redeemed me from the power of sin and made me spiritually alive. But I now know and believe that it has done far more than that. The power of Your blood has made me both able and worthy to know You intimately. It is now appropriate to know You as a friend. To hear Your voice. To receive Your wisdom. To walk through my days with You. Thank you.

The cup of blessing which we bless, is it not the communion of the blood of Christ? The bread which we break, is it not the communion of the body of Christ?

1 CORINTHIANS 10:16

CHAPTER EIGHT

Rightly Discerning the Body of Jesus Encounter

So . . . what's the catch?

Have you ever asked that before? It's a question we've been trained to ask over the years, isn't it? When something sounds too good to be true, we assume that it is.

This skepticism can creep into the church too. For many, there is a skepticism, a wariness, even when they think about the sacrament of Communion.

We've talked about some life-altering, transformational encounters that happen at the Lord's Table — our new covenant in His blood, unity in the body of Christ, the veil of separation being forever torn, the Passover healing, and intimate fellowship with Jesus.

And it is all bought and paid for by the perfect sacrifice of our Savior. We can't earn it, and we can't disqualify ourselves from it. The only thing we have to do is receive and rest in His finished work.

It sounds too good to be true. *Is God really that good? Is it less of a duty and more of a blessing? Is Communion really that powerful? There has got to be something I have to do.*

So . . . what's the catch?

There are those who misinterpret the apostle Paul's words in 1 Corinthians 11:29–30 and falsely think their skepticism is rewarded. Paul writes:

> For he who eats and drinks in an unworthy manner eats and drinks judgment to himself, not discerning the LORD's body. For this

reason many are weak and sick among you, and many sleep.

Aha! There's the catch. We have to be worthy, or we'll bring judgment on ourselves. I knew there was a catch. I knew this was too good to be true.

For this reason, many teach that if there is a sin we have forgotten to confess, then we are unworthy and we are taking Communion in an unworthy manner. Their conclusion is that Paul was saying we are bringing judgment upon ourselves.

First of all, let's remember that there is no part of our salvation and our relationship with God that is possible because we were or are "worthy."

It's never about how perfect we are (because we can never be perfect) — every part of our salvation is about how perfect Jesus was. 2 Corinthians 5:21 says:

For He made Him who knew no sin to be sin for us, that we might become the righteousness of God in Him.

Because of the perfect work of Jesus, we can now freely receive an *"abundance of grace"* and the *"gift of righteousness"* that comes with our salvation (Romans 5:17).

When we read 1 Corinthians 11, taking Communion in an unworthy manner is not about failing to confess a sin; it's about not rightly discerning the Lord's Body. It's about missing an opportunity to receive His goodness.

At the Lord's Table, our focus shouldn't be on ourselves — that's self-righteousness.

In the Communion encounter, we make the choice to put our focus squarely on Jesus — to rightly discern His body. It's to remember His finished work that provided for our healing, our redemption, and our righteousness before God through Christ.

Even though it's healthy to always be repentant, Communion is not a call to repentance. Communion is an invitation to renewal and to celebrate the perfection of Jesus.

The body of Jesus was broken, and His blood was shed so that we could live in health — spiritual, emotional, and physical. Not because we're worthy, but because He is worthy, and He loves us.

> But He was wounded for our transgressions, He was bruised for our iniquities; the chastisement for our peace was upon Him, and by His stripes we are healed. Isaiah 53:5

When you take the bread and the cup in Communion, don't be misled into believing that you are not worthy. Don't believe the lie that you have to confess every sin you can think of before you receive from Him.

Even though it's healthy to always be repentant, Communion is not a call to repentance. Communion is an invitation to renewal and to celebrate the perfection of Jesus. It's remembering that you are clothed in His righteousness.

It is His righteousness that provides redemption, restoration, blessing, favor, wisdom, peace, joy, health, and wholeness. Your role is to believe, to recognize what He has done for you, and to receive what He freely provides.

There is no such thing as "too good to be true" as a new covenant believer. His goodness far outweighs your earthly mind's ability to grasp the depths of His goodness. Everything God has promised, He provides. His goodness knows no limit.

There's never a "catch" with grace.

 **Prayer**

Father, I am so grateful that my emotional, physical, and mental well-being is not dependent upon myself. Because of the work of Jesus on the cross, I can receive spiritual, emotional, and physical renewal and supernatural health. I take my eyes off of myself, and I look to Jesus today to receive every good thing You have provided for me and for my family. I am worthy and righteous because You are worthy and righteous. And I am clothed in the righteousness of Your Son, Jesus Christ. Thank You for Your healing power in my life. I receive it by faith.

Declaration

Jesus, as I take this bread, I *see* You. I see that it represents not only Your broken body but also the finished work accomplished through Your suffering and Your sacrifice. I discern Your presence not only with me and in me, but also in the believers around me . . . Your body. Jesus, I discern Your body in this holy moment, and I remember that Your body was broken so I may be whole.

Jesus, as I take this cup, I rejoice and give thanks for the too-good-to-be-true reality that Your blood sealed a new and better covenant for me . . . one based on better promises. Because of Your blood, I receive Your righteousness; and therefore, I qualify for restoration, blessing, favor, wisdom, peace, joy, health, and wholeness.

Let the word of Christ dwell in you richly in all wisdom, teaching and admonishing one another in psalms and hymns and spiritual songs, singing with grace in your hearts to the Lord.

COLOSSIANS 3:16

CHAPTER NINE

Worshiping Jesus Encounter

There are small details in the Bible, nuances almost, that if we are not careful, we can miss.

Sometimes it's just one verse, or maybe even just a phrase within the verse. But it's there for a reason.

This is why reading the Word of God should never be done out of duty or just to check off a box on our spiritual to-do list. Instead, so much encouragement and wisdom come when we meditate on the inspired words we find in Scripture.

The writer of Hebrews tells us in Hebrews 4:12:

The word of God is living and powerful, and sharper than any two-edged sword, piercing even to the division of soul and spirit, and of joints and marrow, and is a discerner of the thoughts and intents of the heart.

God's Word is alive. It teaches, corrects, exhorts, comforts, encourages, reminds, and transforms us. Every single word.

In Matthew's Gospel and in Mark's Gospel, we find one of these small details that would be easy to miss . . . but it does reveal to us another incredible encounter that happens in Communion.

It's just one verse. But a verse that can transform you today.

Immediately after Jesus and His disciples had shared Communion, they did something else. Something we hadn't seen in any other place in the Gospels.

Matthew 26:30 says:

And when they had sung a hymn, they went out to the Mount of Olives.

And Mark 14:26 says the exact same thing. What a picture! Jesus and His disciples worshiping God at the Lord's Table.

Those simple seven words — *"And when they had sung a hymn"* — show us that Communion is a worship encounter. Jesus demonstrated it for us. We simply have to see it.

We don't have to wait until we are in a church service to worship. We don't have to wait for a praise band to lead us. One of the most personal, intimate places to worship is when we remember the sacrifice of Jesus and all that it gives us.

There are many reasons to worship God, but one of the most powerful reasons is to be thankful for who He is and what He has done to rescue us.

The psalmist surely had this truth in mind when writing Psalm 40:

> I waited patiently for the LORD; he turned to me and heard my cry. He lifted me out of the slimy pit, out of the mud and mire; he set my feet on a rock and gave me a firm place to stand. He put a new song in my mouth, a hymn of praise to our God. Many will see and fear the LORD and put their trust in him.
> Psalm 40:1-3, NIV

Notice that being delivered from destruction results in having *"a new song"* in our mouths. A *"hymn of praise"* to God.

Taking Communion is not just an opportunity to remember all that Jesus provided for us, but to stop, give thanks, and worship Him for it — to pause in reverence and awe at His mercy, goodness, and loving-kindness.

Whether you are taking Holy Communion in your living room, in a hospital room, in a church

Taking Communion is not just an opportunity to remember all that Jesus provided for us, but to stop, give thanks, and worship Him for it — to pause in reverence and awe at His mercy, goodness, and loving-kindness.

service, or in your car on your way to work — let it be a holy moment. Let it be a time of worship.

Pour out your heart to Jesus and thank Him for His sacrifice. Thank Him for His salvation, His healing, His righteousness, His freedom, and His peace and joy.

The example Scripture gives us in one short verse tells us so much. And it's there for a reason. It's just a few short words, but it gives us a powerful reminder . . .

Communion is an opportunity to encounter Jesus through worship.

 **Prayer**

Father, I worship You. You are the Creator of the Universe, the God of miracles, my redeemer, my savior, my friend. There is nothing You cannot do; nothing is impossible for You. I praise You not only for what You have done; I praise You for what You are doing and what You will continue to do in my life. My future is filled with good things because You are with me. Every day I will worship You with a heart of thankfulness.

Declaration

I take this bread and am filled with awe and grateful wonder as I consider all Jesus accomplished for me through His broken body. As I ponder what that sacrifice has done for me and in me, I can only raise my hands in worship of Your majesty and amazing love.

I drink this cup and lift my voice in praise and worship to the One who has forgiven my sins and made all things new in my life. You have heard my cry and lifted me out of the pit of destruction. You have put a new song in my mouth, a hymn of praise and gratitude for the rescue your precious, sinless blood purchased for me.

"God is Spirit, and those who worship Him must worship in spirit and truth."

JOHN 4:24

CHAPTER TEN

Marriage Supper Encounter

At the Passover meal, when Jesus instituted the Lord's Supper, just hours before He would go to the cross for our healing and forgiveness, He made a promise:

> And as they were eating, Jesus took bread, blessed and broke it, and gave it to the disciples and said, "Take, eat; this is My body." Then He took the cup, and gave thanks, and gave it to them, saying, "Drink from it, all of you. For this is My blood of the new covenant, which is shed for many for the remission of sins. But I say to you, I will not drink of this fruit of the vine from now on until that day when I

drink it new with you in my Father's kingdom."
Matthew 26:26–29

Can you see the picture of this promise in your mind's eye?

Jesus, our perfect Savior, sits at the right hand of God in a position of rest, because His work is finished, and He is waiting to have dinner with you in His Father's kingdom.

It's quite a picture, isn't it? A celebration in Heaven. A dinner like nothing we've ever imagined. A party planned and hosted by the King of Kings.

And here is the truly amazing thing: you and I have a seat at the table. No shame. No fear. No regret. Just celebrating the goodness of our heavenly Father and receiving His love in unbroken fellowship.

When we take Communion, it is an opportunity to remember all that Jesus has provided through

His work on the cross. But that provision isn't *only* past tense. And it isn't *only* present tense.

Yes, He has healed us and made a way for us in the past. We can look back and see His hand in victories. And, yes, He is working on our behalf even today — His mercies are new every morning.

But the body of Jesus that was broken for us and the blood of Jesus that was shed for us, has made the way for an eternity to be spent in His presence. There will be no more pain, no more tears, no more suffering. But rather joy, worship, fellowship, contentment, and celebration.

We see the love of God all throughout Scripture. We see it in His fellowship in the garden. We see it in the miracles, prophecies, and shadows in the Old Testament. We see it in the life of Jesus. He was grace and truth — the fulfillment of the law. His love established a new and better covenant.

But perhaps we see God's love most clearly at His table. A time when we remember that Jesus lived, died, and rose from the grave so that we would never be separated from God again.

He loves us and He wants to be with us.

Emmanuel — God with us. Today, tomorrow, and forever. This is what we encounter when we take the bread and drink the cup. A celebration that He is waiting to enjoy with us.

Blessed are those who are called to the marriage supper of the Lamb (Revelation 19:9).

Jesus, our perfect Savior, sits at the right hand of God in a position of rest, because His work is finished, and He is waiting to have dinner with you in His Father's kingdom.

 **Prayer**

Father, I thank You for the promise of Heaven. Because of the finished work of Jesus, I have fellowship with You as my guarantee for eternity. Cause me to remember how much You love me and that You will never leave me. When I face troubles in this world, I know they are temporal. I look to You because I know You have overcome the world. You were with me yesterday. You are here with me today, and it's just the beginning. I have an eternity to enjoy with You, to worship You, and to receive Your abundance planned for me.

Declaration

Jesus, I take this bread, recognizing that I have a seat at the most important table that has ever been, or ever will be, set — Your heavenly wedding feast. Your body, broken for me, has made it possible for me to dine with you daily and partake of your goodness. You have also prepared a table before me in the presence of my enemies. Surely Your goodness and mercy follow me all my days.

I drink this cup, knowing that the wine served at the marriage supper of the Lamb, where I am an eternal guest, is the wine of forgiveness, the wine of gladness, and the wine of joy. I recline at rest at the King's banquet table, at complete rest from my striving to qualify for favor, blessing, and acceptance. By the blood of the Lamb, I overcome!

Have you been to the Cross?

It's possible that none of the special encounters in this book had meaning or power for you because you've never appropriated Jesus' extraordinary sacrifice to your life. You do that by simply receiving the Father's free gift of salvation and eternal life, made possible through Jesus' sacrifice.

Jesus didn't just die for you. He died as you. He died on the cross in your place. In His death, He took on all the bad you deserve, so you could receive all the good and blessing and life He deserved. Once you make the choice to receive that gift, nothing will ever be the same for you again.

Are you ready to receive the free and limitless gift of salvation through Jesus Christ? If so, pray this prayer:

Father in Heaven, I recognize that I can't reach You or Heaven on my own. I have nothing to offer. Nothing to give. So I come to the cross of Jesus now to receive Your free, gracious gift of forgiveness, cleansing, and eternal life.

Right now, take my guilt, my shame, my brokenness and lay it upon Jesus' cross. I gratefully receive this amazing gift with gratitude and joy. Thank you!

Did you pray that prayer? Here's good news. Romans 10:13 says: "Everyone who calls on the Lord's name will experience new life." (TPT)

Congratulations!

The Great Exchange

Communion points us to the cross. And the cross is a place of exchange. There, through Jesus' extraordinary sacrifice, we are invited to bring our sin, our shame, our sickness, and every other vile aspect of the curse, lay them down, and walk away with everything blessed that Jesus is and has. What an opportunity.

May your communion encounters remind you of all Jesus purchased for you and bring into ever fuller possession of them in your life.

Take Communion

Find additional resources and testimonies at
TakeCommunion.com

Notes

[i] Brennan Manning, *The Ragamuffin Gospel* (Colorado Springs: Multnomah, 1990) 91